CAMBRIDGE PRIMARY
Science

Challenge 1

Jon Board and Alan Cross

CAMBRIDGE UNIVERSITY PRESS

CAMBRIDGE
UNIVERSITY PRESS

University Printing House, Cambridge CB2 8BS, United Kingdom

One Liberty Plaza, 20th Floor, New York, NY 10006, USA

477 Williamstown Road, Port Melbourne, VIC 3207, Australia

314–321, 3rd Floor, Plot 3, Splendor Forum, Jasola District Centre, New Delhi – 110025, India

79 Anson Road, #06–04/06, Singapore 079906

Cambridge University Press is part of the University of Cambridge.

It furthers the University's mission by disseminating knowledge in the pursuit of education, learning and research at the highest international levels of excellence.

www.cambridge.org
Information on this title: www.cambridge.org/9781316611135

© Cambridge University Press 2016

This publication is in copyright. Subject to statutory exception and to the provisions of relevant collective licensing agreements, no reproduction of any part may take place without the written permission of Cambridge University Press.

First published 2016

20　19　18　17　16　15　14　13　12　11　10　9　8

Produced for Cambridge University Press by
White-Thomson Publishing
www.wtpub.co.uk

Editor: Rachel Minay
Designer: Tracey Camden

Printed in India by Repro India Ltd

A catalogue record for this publication is available from the British Library

ISBN 978-1-316-61113-5 Paperback

Additional resources for this publication at www.cambridge.org/

Cambridge University Press has no responsibility for the persistence or accuracy of URLs for external or third-party internet websites referred to in this publication, and does not guarantee that any content on such websites is, or will remain, accurate or appropriate. Information regarding prices, travel timetables, and other factual information given in this work is correct at the time of first printing but Cambridge University Press does not guarantee the accuracy of such information thereafter.

Cover artwork: Bill Bolton

NOTICE TO TEACHERS IN THE UK

It is illegal to reproduce any part of this work in material form (including photocopying and electronic storage) except under the following circumstances:
(i) where you are abiding by a licence granted to your school or institution by the Copyright Licensing Agency;
(ii) where no such licence exists, or where you wish to exceed the terms of a licence, and you have gained the written permission of Cambridge University Press;
(iii) where you are allowed to reproduce without permission under the provisions of Chapter 3 of the Copyright, Designs and Patents Act 1988, which covers, for example, the reproduction of short passages within certain types of educational anthology and reproduction for the purposes of setting examination questions.

Contents

Introduction	**4**
1 Being alive	**5**
1.2 Local environments	6
1.3 Animal babies	8
1.4 Healthy food and drink	10
2 Growing plants	**11**
2.1 Plant life cycle	12
2.2 Growing seeds	15
2.3 Plants and light	17
3 Ourselves	**19**
3.1 We are similar	20
3.2 We are different	22
3.3 Our bodies	23
3.4 Our fantastic senses	25
4 Materials in my world	**27**
4.1 What is it made of?	28
4.2 Using materials	30
4.3 Sorting materials	32
5 Pushes and pulls	**34**
5.3 Pushes and pulls around us	35
5.4 Changing movement	37
6 Hearing sounds	**39**
6.1 Where do sounds come from?	40
6.2 Our ears	41
Answers	**43**
Glossary	**48**

Introduction

This series of primary science activity books complements *Cambridge Primary Science* and progresses, through practice, learner confidence and depth of knowledge in the skills of scientific enquiry (SE) and key scientific vocabulary and concepts. These activity books will:

- enhance and extend learners' scientific knowledge and facts
- promote scientific enquiry skills and learning in order to think like a scientist
- advance each learner's knowledge and use of scientific vocabulary and concepts in their correct context.

The *Challenge* activity books extend learners' understanding of the main curriculum, providing an opportunity to increase the depth of their knowledge and scientific enquiry skills from a key selection of topics. This workbook does not cover all of the curriculum framework content for this stage.

How to use the activity books

These activity books have been designed for use by individual learners, either in the classroom or at home. As teachers and as parents, you can decide how and when they are used by your learner to best improve their progress. The *Challenge* activity books target specific topics (lessons) from Grades 1–6 from all the units covered in *Cambridge Primary Science*. This targeted approach has been carefully designed to consolidate topics where help is most needed.

How to use the units

Unit introduction

Each unit starts with an introduction for you as the teacher or parent. It clearly sets out which topics are covered in the unit and the learning objectives of the activities in each section. This is where you can work with learners to select all, most or just one of the sections according to individual needs.

The introduction also provides advice and tips on how best to support the learner in the skills of scientific enquiry and in the practice of key scientific vocabulary.

At this grade, it is very likely the learners are still learning to read, so teacher/parent may need to explain these verbally.

Sections

Each section matches a corresponding lesson in the main series. Sections contain write-in activities that are supported by:

- Key words – key vocabulary for the topic, also highlighted in bold in the sections
- Key facts – a short fact to support the activities where relevant
- Look and learn – where needed, activities are supported with scientific exemplars for extra support of how to treat a concept or scientific method
- Remember – tips for the learner to steer them in the right direction.

How to approach the write-in activities

Teachers and parents are advised to provide students with a blank A5 notebook at the start of each grade for learners to use alongside these activity books. Most activities will provide enough space for the answers required. However, some learner responses – especially to enquiry-type questions – may require more space for notes. Keeping notes and plans models how scientists work and encourages learners to explore and record their thinking, leaving the activity books for the final, more focused answers.

Think about it questions

Each unit also contains some questions for discussion at home with parents, or at school. Although learners will record the outcomes of their discussions in the activity book, these questions are intended to encourage the students to think more deeply.

Self-assessment

Each section in the unit ends with a self-assessment opportunity for learners: empty circles with short learning statements. Teachers or parents can ask learners to complete the circles in a number of ways, depending on their age and preference, e.g. with faces, traffic light colours or numbers. The completed self-assessments provide teachers with a clearer understanding of how best to progress and support individual learners.

Glossary of key words and concepts

At the end of each activity book there is a glossary of key scientific words and concepts arranged by unit. Learners are regularly reminded to practise saying these words out loud and in sentences to improve communication skills in scientific literacy.

1 Being alive

The unit challenge

The activities in this Challenge unit will extend learners' knowledge of the following topics in the Learner's Book and Activity Book:

Topic	In this topic, learners will:
1.1 Animals and plants alive!	see Skills Builder, Section 1.1
1.2 Local environments	compare animals and plants in two local environments
1.3 Animal babies	collect evidence by measuring using non-standard units
1.4 Healthy food and drink	sort healthy and unhealthy drinks

Help your learner

In this unit, learners will answer questions by collecting evidence through exploring and observing (Sections 1.2 and 1.3). They will also start to make comparisons (Sections 1.2, 1.3 and 1.4). To help them:

1 Look up the names of the animals and plants learners find with them and help them as they label their drawings.

2 In Section 1.3, help learners to research how mice grow in more detail using books or the internet.

⚠️ Learners will need adult help in Section 1.2 to keep them safe.

TEACHING TIP
Remember, learners can also use their notebooks.

1.2 Local environments

magnifying glass, environment, plant, animal, name, compare

Different environments

You will need a **magnifying glass**.

1 **Choose two different environments.**

You can choose anywhere outdoors. Ask an adult to help you.

⚠ Only look in safe places. Look out for plants that sting or animals that bite.

You can choose a wall.

You can choose a flower pot or flowerbed.

2 What **plants** and **animals** can you find? Use the magnifying glass to look for very small animals.

3 **Draw and name the plants and animals you find in each environment.**

Environment 1: _____
Plants	Animals

Environment 2: _____
Plants	Animals

4 **Think about it!**

Which environment had more plants? _____

CHECK YOUR LEARNING

○ I can look closely and **compare** environments.

1.3 Animal babies

baby, mouse, kitten, grow, long, food, young

LOOK AND LEARN

A **baby mouse** is called a '**kitten**'.
A baby cat is also called a 'kitten'.

Measure the mouse

Look at this mouse kitten as it **grows**.

1 Colour the bricks to show how many bricks **long** the mouse is.

	Length of the mouse
2 weeks old	_____ bricks
4 weeks old	_____ bricks

1.3 Animal babies

7 weeks old	_____ bricks
10 weeks old	_____ bricks

2 Think about it!

What does a mouse kitten do as it grows?
Tick all the correct boxes ✓.

gets longer?	yes ☐	no ☐
grows more fur?	yes ☐	no ☐
eats more **food**?	yes ☐	no ☐

CHECK YOUR LEARNING

◯ I can use bricks to compare length.

◯ I know that **young** animals grow larger as they get older.

1 Being alive

1.4 Healthy food and drink

healthy, drink, sugar, unhealthy

Healthy and unhealthy drinks

1 Draw arrows to put the **healthy drinks** into Ali's shopping basket.

LOOK AND LEARN

Some drinks contain lots of **sugar**. Too much sugar is **unhealthy**.

2 Think about it!

Which drinks are the healthiest?

_____

CHECK YOUR LEARNING

◯ I know which drinks are healthy.

Remember:

Fruit juice has lots of sugar but also has healthy things called vitamins. It is good to drink some fruit juice, but not too much.

2 Growing plants

The unit challenge

The activities in this Challenge unit will extend learners' knowledge of the following topics from the Learner's Book and Activity Book:

Topic	In this topic, learners will:
2.1 Plant life cycle	learn about a plant's life cycle
2.2 Growing seeds	predict whether seeds need water to grow into plants and then find out
2.3 Plants need light	understand that plants need light to grow

Help your learner

In this unit, learners will learn to answer questions by collecting evidence through observation (Sections 2.2 and 2.3) and make predictions and comparisons (Section 2.2). To help them:

1 In Section 2.1, talk about what a life cycle means, and what a 'stage' in a life cycle means.

2 Help learners to grow seeds in Section 2.2. Set up a space where the plant pots can stay undisturbed.

3 Encourage learners to make predictions before they carry out an activity. Explain that predictions don't have to be right – they are like a best guess. Learning from mistakes is an important part of science.

⚠ Remind learners that some plants are poisonous.

TEACHING TIP

Remind learners that the plant world includes everything from tiny plants to huge trees, but that they mostly have the plant parts we are studying.

2.1 Plant life cycle

life cycle, stage, seed, seedling, leaf, roots, flower, fruit

LOOK AND LEARN

This is a **life cycle** of a butterfly. Arrows join up each **stage**.

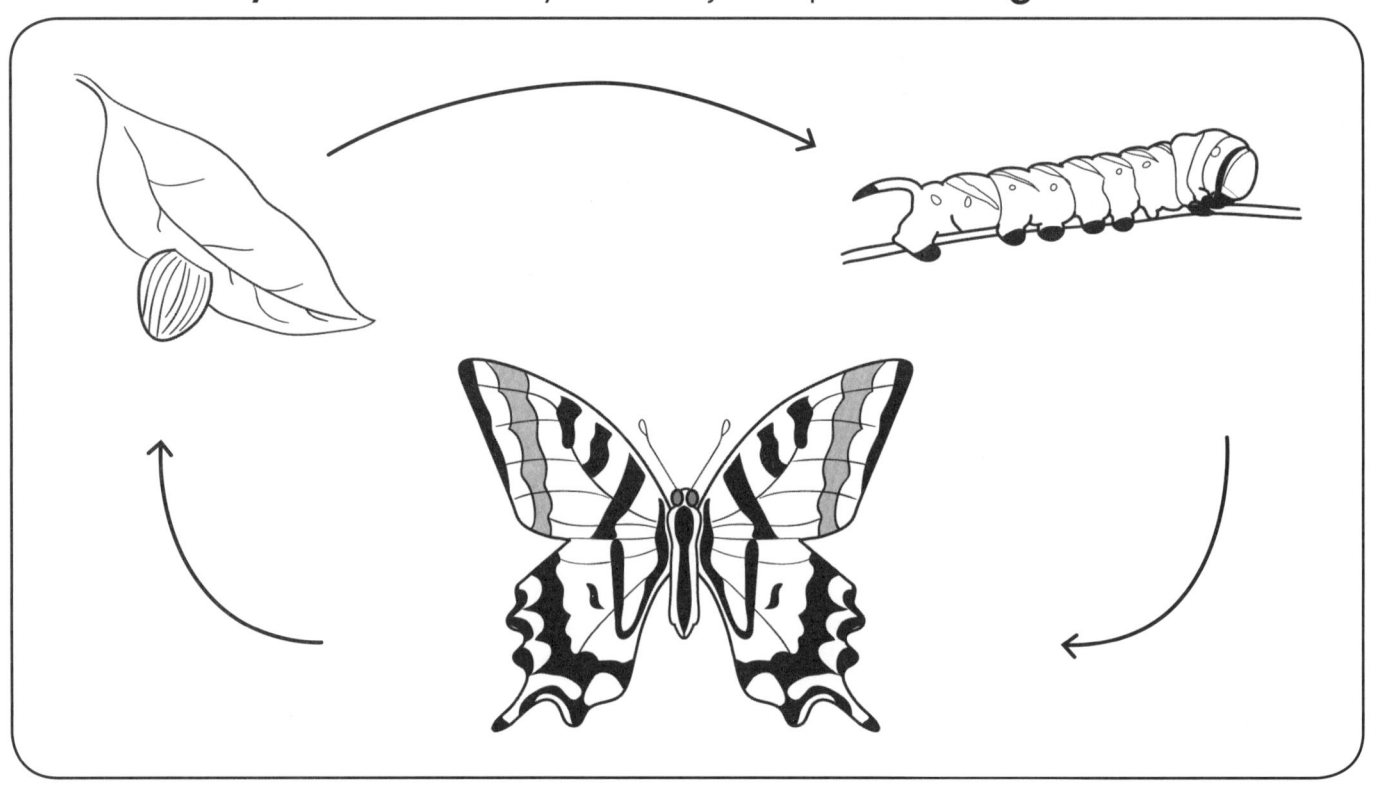

The life cycle of a plant

1. Look at these words. They are all to do with the life cycle of a plant.

> **seed**   plant   **seedling**   **leaves**
> **root**   **flower**   seed pod

2 Add arrows between these pictures to show the plant's life cycle.

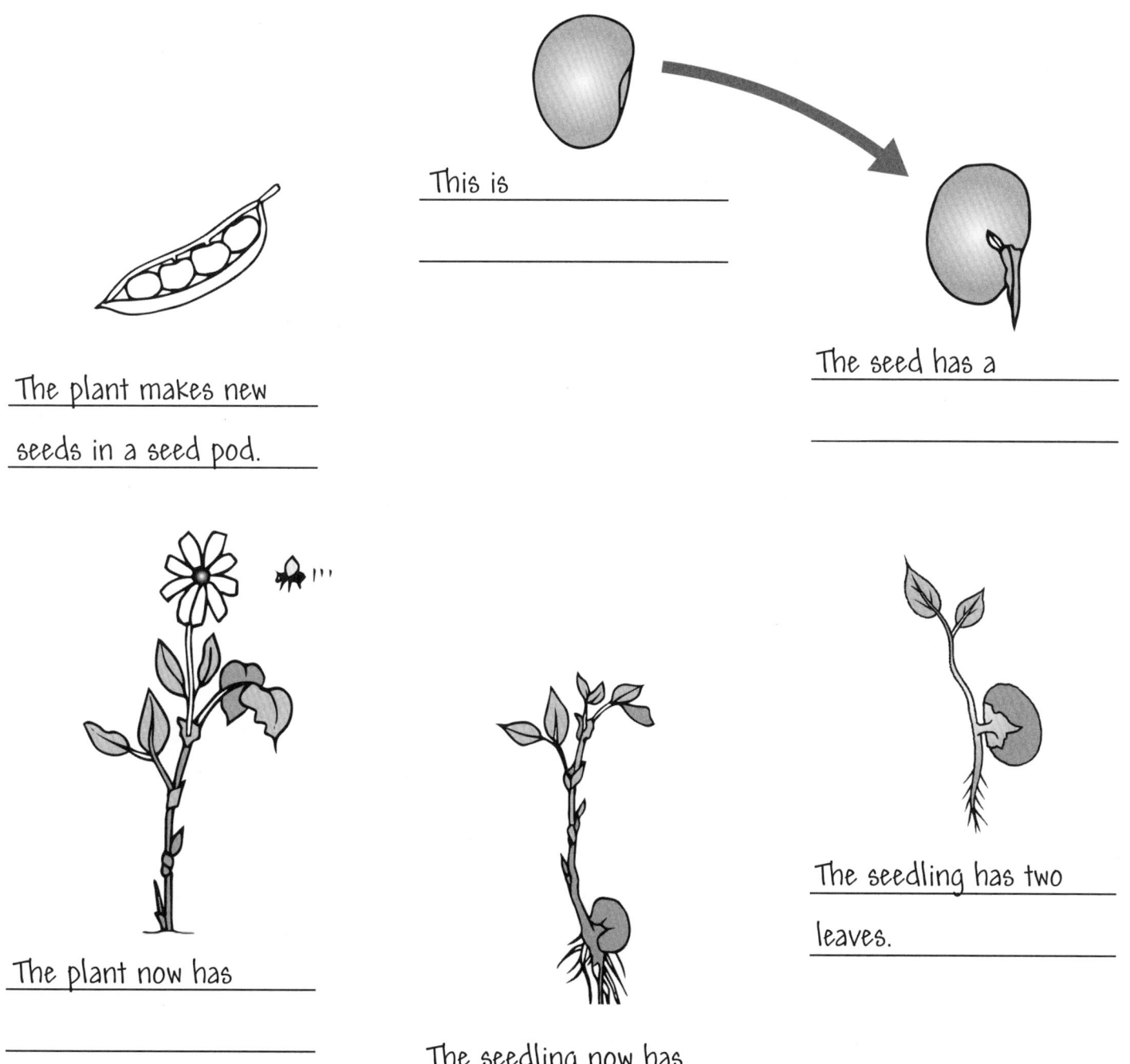

This is _____

The seed has a _____

The plant makes new seeds in a seed pod.

The seedling has two leaves.

The plant now has _____

The seedling now has _____

3 Finish the sentences to write what is happening in each picture. Use the words in the box in question 1 to help you.

Plant foods

Some plant parts are safe to eat. Draw and name a plant food you eat in each of the shapes below.

Remember: When you look at a plant, think about the shape, size and colour of the leaves. Some plants have flowers and **fruit**.

Leaf

⚠ Remember that some plants are poisonous.

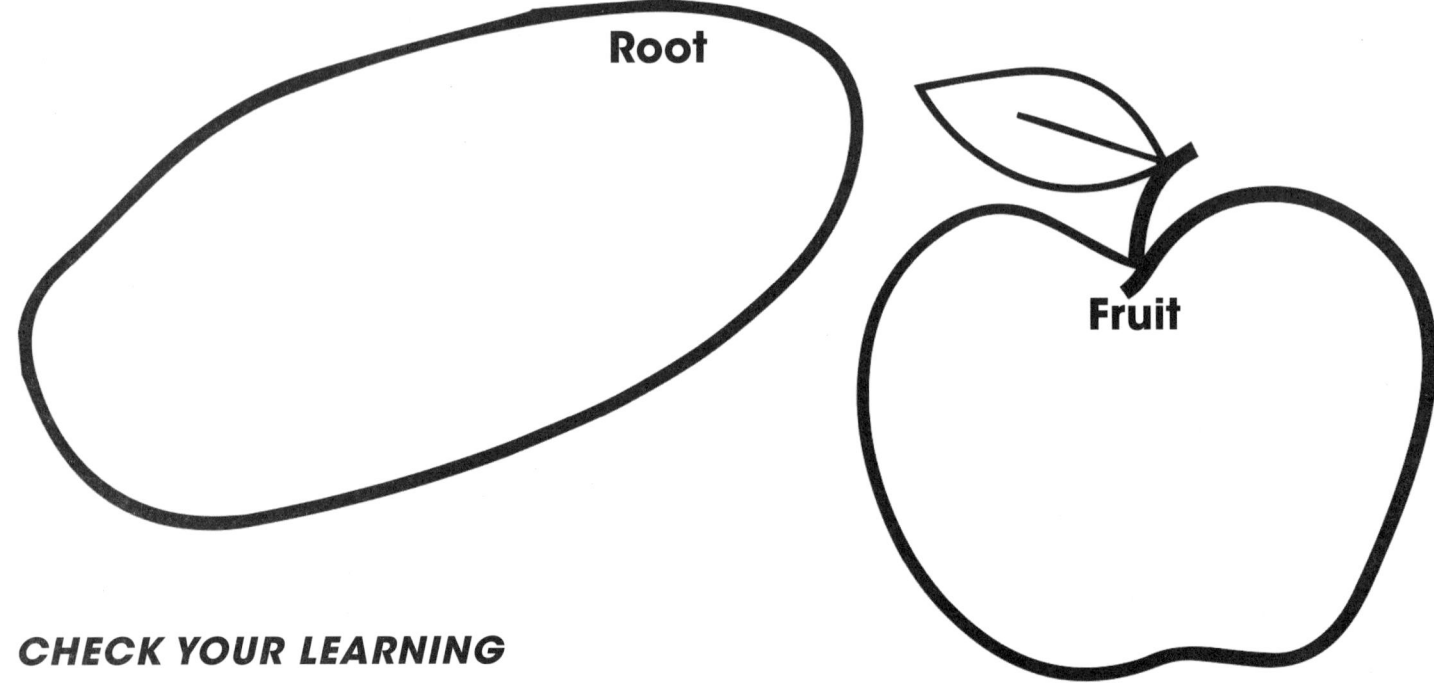

Root

Fruit

CHECK YOUR LEARNING

○ I know that plants have roots and leaves and some have flowers and fruit.

○ I know that plants grow and make flowers and seed.

2.1 Plant life cycle

2.2 Growing seeds

water, feel

Do seeds need water?

You will need three plant pots, soil and seeds.

1 Sow five seeds in each pot.

2 Put no **water** in Pot 1.

Give Pot 2 one teaspoon of water every day.

Water Pot 3 when the soil **feels** dry.

3 What do you think will happen? Tick the boxes ✓.

	grow	not grow
Pot 1	☐	☐
Pot 2	☐	☐
Pot 3	☐	☐

4 Which pot will grow best? _____

Why? _____

5 Wait for the seeds to start growing. Then draw your results over a number of days in this table.

Day	Pot 1 No water	Pot 2 A little water	Pot 3 Water when needed

6 Which plants grew the best? Why?

_____

_____

CHECK YOUR LEARNING

◯ I know that plants need water to grow.

Remember:

Plants need water, but not too much. If you give them too much water, they may die.

2.2 Growing seeds

2.3 Plants and light

light

Do plants need light?

You will need three plants.

1 Izumi has grown these plants. Join a label to each plant to show where they were grown.

Grown in the dark

Grown in a shady place

Grown in the light

2 Now grow a plant in the dark and a plant in the light.
Draw what you will do.

1 I will grow a plant in the dark:

2 I will grow a plant in the light:

3 Look at your plants each day. What do you see?

_____

_____

_____

CHECK YOUR LEARNING

○ I know that plants need light to grow.

3 Ourselves

The unit challenge

The activities in this Challenge unit will extend learners' knowledge of the following topics from the Learner's Book and Activity Book:

Topic	In this topic, learners will:
3.1 We are similar	think about what makes us similar
3.2 We are different	understand that we are all different in some ways
3.3 Our bodies	name and count the main parts of the body
3.4 Our fantastic senses	learn about the senses and test their friends' ability to identify different sounds

Help your learner

In this unit learners will collect evidence to answer questions (Sections 3.1, 3.3 and 3.4), decide what to do to answer a science question (Section 3.4) and make comparisons (Sections 3.1 and 3.2). They will also make predictions and compare what happened with their predictions (Section 3.4). To help them:

1 Allow learners to plan as much of each activity as possible. Help learners when they need it.

2 Encourage learners to develop an interest in keeping their body healthy.

⚠ In Section 3.4, remind learners that very loud sounds could damage their ears.

TEACHING TIP
Encourage learners to use the words to describe the senses. Talk together about your senses and the senses of other people and animals.

3 Ourselves

3.1 We are similar

similar, pictogram

We like similar things

1 Talk to your friends about things that make you **similar**. Fill in the boxes.

We have similar bodies.	We like similar foods.
We all have ears.	
We like similar games.	We like similar stories.

2 What other things do you all like?

_____

Healthy food we love

1 Look at the **pictogram**. It shows how many children liked these fruits.

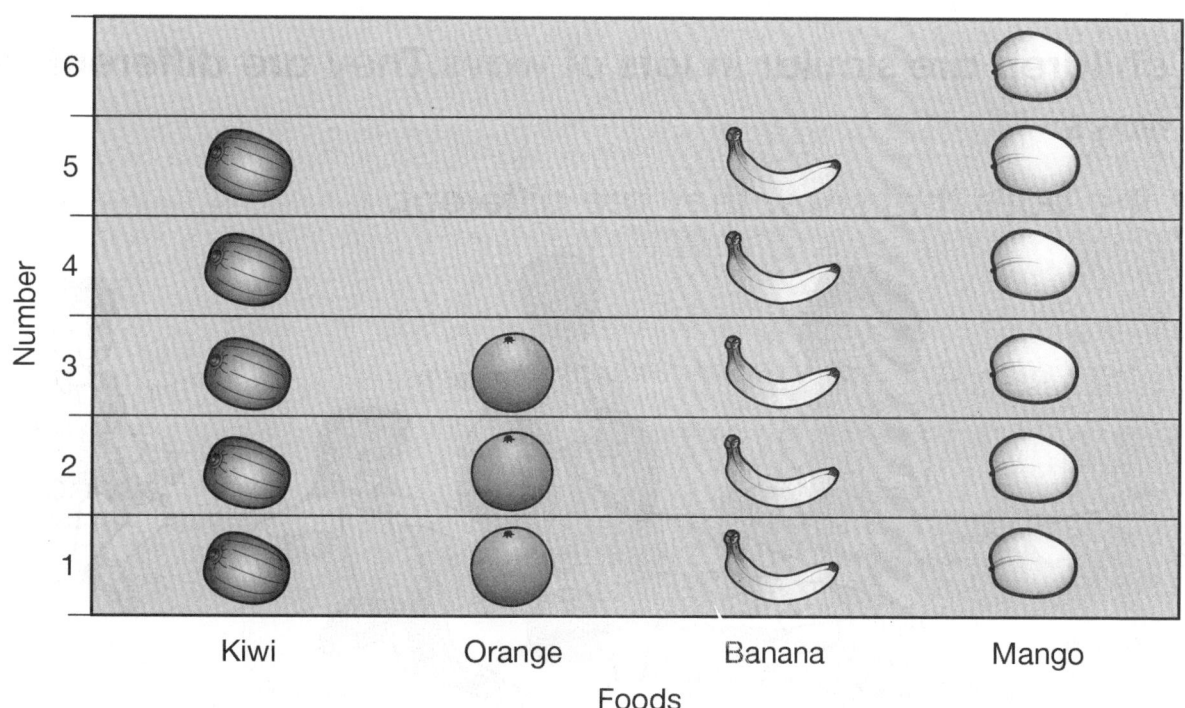

2 Which is the most popular fruit? _____

3 Which is the least popular fruit? _____

4 Two fruits got the same score. Which fruits?

_____ and _____

5 **Think about it!**

You are similar to your friends and to children in other countries. Do you think all people are similar?

_____

CHECK YOUR LEARNING

◯   I know that we are similar in lots of ways.

3.2 We are different

different

Children are different

These children are similar in lots of ways. They are **different** in some ways.

Colour the balls that show they are different.

We have different hair.

We all have a mouth.

Some of us are tall.

We all love basketball.

Remember: We are all different in some ways.

CHECK YOUR LEARNING

 I know that we are all different in some ways.

3.3 Our bodies

Spot our body parts!

Look, the children have crashed.

> body, head, hair, eye, ear, mouth, nose, shoulder, arm, fingers, hand, knee, leg, toes, foot

⚠️ Always take care on your bicycle. Always wear a helmet.

3 Ourselves 23

1 Point to all of these **body** parts on the picture:

| head | hair | eye | ear |

| mouth | nose | shoulder |

| arm | fingers | hand | knee |

| leg | toes | foot |

2 Look at the picture and only count the parts you can actually see.

a How many heads can you see? _____

b How many hands can you see? _____

c How many fingers can you see? _____

3 Think about it!

Look in a mirror. How many parts of your face and head can you name? Write them in this box.

CHECK YOUR LEARNING

○ I can name many body parts.

3.3 Our bodies

3.4 Our fantastic senses

senses, hear, see, smell, touch, tongue, taste

What is this sound?

You will need three friends, a blindfold, paper, keys and three other objects that make a sound.

LOOK AND LEARN

Our **senses** tell us about the world around us. We use our ears to **hear**, our eyes to **see**, our nose to **smell**, our skin to **touch**, and our **tongue** to **taste**.

Can your friends name different sounds?

3 Ourselves
25

1 Look at the table. Choose three more sounds and write them in.

Sound	My friend _____	My friend _____	My friend _____
tearing paper	yes / no	yes / no	yes / no
shaking keys	yes / no	yes / no	yes / no
	yes / no	yes / no	yes / no
	yes / no	yes / no	yes / no
	yes / no	yes / no	yes / no

2 Which sound do you think will be hardest to name?

_____

3 Ask your friend to wear a blindfold and carry out the sound test.

4 Repeat for your other friends.

5 Did any children get all the sounds right?

_____

6 Which sound was hardest to name? Were you right?

_____

> ⚠ Take care. Very loud sounds can damage your ears.

> **Remember:**
> You can do this at school with the teacher's help.

CHECK YOUR LEARNING

◯ I know that our senses tell us about the world around us.

3.4 Our fantastic senses

4 Materials in my world

The unit challenge

The activities in this Challenge unit will extend learners' knowledge of the following topics from the Learner's Book and Activity Book:

Topic	In this topic, learners will:
4.1 What is it made of?	name many common materials, including wood, glass, plastic, paper, metal, concrete and fabric
4.2 Using materials	recognise that different materials have different properties understand that materials with different properties are used for different jobs
4.3 Sorting materials	sort materials into two groups using a magnet

Help your learner

In this unit, learners will collect evidence to answer questions (Sections 4.1 and 4.2), suggest ideas and follow instructions (Sections 4.1 and 4.2). They will also make predictions and record stages in work (Section 4.3). To help them:

1 Ask learners to explain what they observe. Ask questions that begin with why, what and how.

TEACHING TIP
Talk with learners about why different materials are used for different jobs.

TEACHING TIP
Materials are usually made into objects. Encourage learners to talk about the properties of the material rather than the object. For example a towel is made of soft cotton, an iron is made of strong metal.

4.1 What is it made of?

> materials, paper, fabric, metal, plastic, wood, rock, rubber, glass, concrete

Materials all around

1 Look around the room. Can you find three objects made from each **material** below?

paper
1. _____wallpaper_____
2. _____
3. _____

fabric
1. _____
2. _____
3. _____

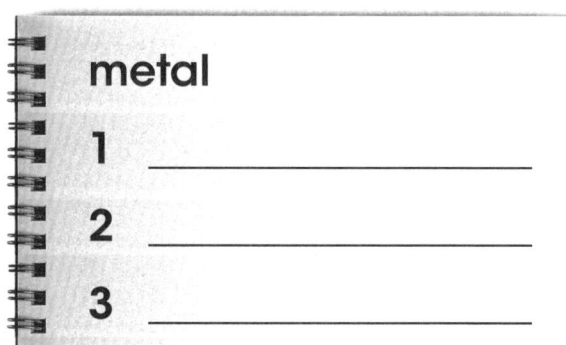

metal
1. _____
2. _____
3. _____

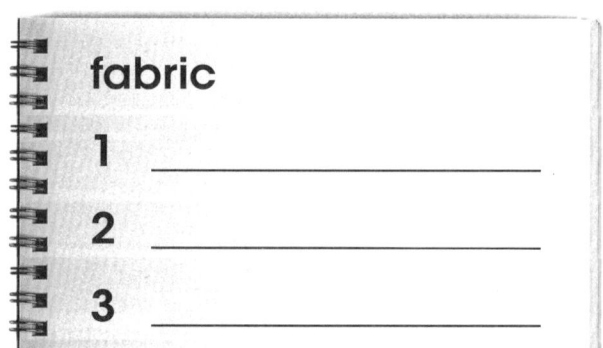

Remember:
Remember to look carefully. You will see lots of different materials!

2 Can you think of an object made from these materials?

plastic　　　＿＿＿＿＿＿＿＿＿＿＿＿＿

wood　　　　＿＿＿＿＿＿＿＿＿＿＿＿＿

rock　　　　＿＿＿＿＿＿＿＿＿＿＿＿＿

rubber　　　＿＿＿＿＿＿＿＿＿＿＿＿＿

glass　　　　＿＿＿＿＿＿＿＿＿＿＿＿＿

concrete　　＿＿＿＿＿＿＿＿＿＿＿＿＿

> **KEY FACT**
>
> Animals use materials too. Lots of animals and birds make nests. A gorilla will make a nest of leaves.

3 **Think about it!**

What is the best material in the world? Is it water?

＿＿＿＿＿＿＿＿＿＿＿＿＿＿＿＿＿＿＿＿＿＿＿＿＿＿＿＿＿＿＿＿＿＿＿＿＿＿＿

CHECK YOUR LEARNING

○　I know that there are lots of different materials.

○　I can name common materials including wood, glass, plastic, paper, metal, concrete and fabric.

4 Materials in my world

4.2 Using materials

properties, strong, flexible, soft, rough, smooth, see-through, elastic

Investigating materials

You will need a magnifying glass.

1 Find three different materials. Look at them closely.

2 What are the **properties** of each material? Use these words to help you fill in the table.

KEY FACT

The properties of different materials make them good for different jobs.

strong   flexible   soft   rough   smooth

Material	It feels ...	Through the magnifying glass I can see ...
wood	rough	thin bits of wood

Remember:

When you use a magnifying glass, keep your head still and move the glass.

3 Are any materials cold to touch?

_____

4 Are any materials warm to touch?

_____

5 Are any materials **see-through**? What can you do to find out?

_____

6 Think about it!

Lots of materials you use are **elastic**. Why is rubber good for making rubber bands?

_____

CHECK YOUR LEARNING

○ I know that different materials have different properties.

○ I know that different materials with different properties are used for different jobs.

4.3 Sorting materials

magnet, test, sort

Sorting with a magnet?

You will need a magnet.

Tila is testing materials to see if they are pulled to a magnet.

1 Find some materials to **sort** with a magnet. What do you think will happen? Fill in this box.

I think the magnet will pull these materials
_____
_____
_____
_____
_____

2 Now test your materials.

3 Which are pulled to the magnet? Write your results here.

> **Remember:**
> Use the same magnet for each material so that the test you do is a fair one.

The magnet pulled …

_____

_____

_____

_____

_____

_____

4 **Think about it!**

Riaz has dropped a box of rubber bands and metal paper clips. Can Riaz pick up the paper clips quickly? (Clue: he has a magnet.)

_____

_____

CHECK YOUR LEARNING

◯ I know that materials can be sorted by their properties.

◯ I know that magnets can be used to sort some materials.

5 Pushes and pulls

The unit challenge

The activities in this Challenge unit will extend learners' knowledge of the following topics in the Learner's Book and Activity Book:

Topic	In this topic, learners will:
5.1 In the playground	see Skills Builder, Section 5.1
5.2 How toys work	see Skills Builder, Section 5.2
5.3 Pushes and pulls around us	compare the sizes of pushes and pulls
5.4 Changing movement	investigate the effect of forces on falling paper

Help your learner

In this unit, learners will explore and observe in order to collect evidence to answer questions (Sections 5.3 and 5.4), make comparisons (Sections 5.3 and 5.4), make predictions and compare what happened with their predictions (Section 5.4). To help them:

1 Talk with learners about the 'Think about it!' questions. These will develop their skills of considering evidence.

2 In Topic 5.4, learners may need help to make predictions. Ask them to think about what happens when they drop other objects. They could be further challenged by asking them to give a reason for their prediction.

> ⚠ Make sure that learners do not push or pull things that are too big or heavy and might cause damage to objects and people.

5.3 Pushes and pulls around us

push, pull, move

LOOK AND LEARN Some things need a big **push** or **pull** to make them **move**. Some things need a small push or pull.

Pushes and pulls, big and small

You will need sticky notes.

1 Find some things that need big or small pushes or pulls.

⚠️ Take care. Do not push or pull things that are too big or heavy and might cause damage to objects and people.

2 Use sticky notes to label them 'big push', 'small push', 'big pull' or 'small pull'.

3 Think about it!

Why do big things usually need big pushes or pulls to make them **move**? Tick one box.

because they are big ☐

because they are heavy ☐

CHECK YOUR LEARNING

◯ I can say whether pushes and pulls are big or small.

5.4 Changing movement

predict, fall, fast, slow, gravity

Falling paper

You will need a sheet of paper.

1. **Predict** what you think will happen each time.
2. Drop the paper in different ways.
3. Write what happens. Use these words: **falls fast**   falls **slow**

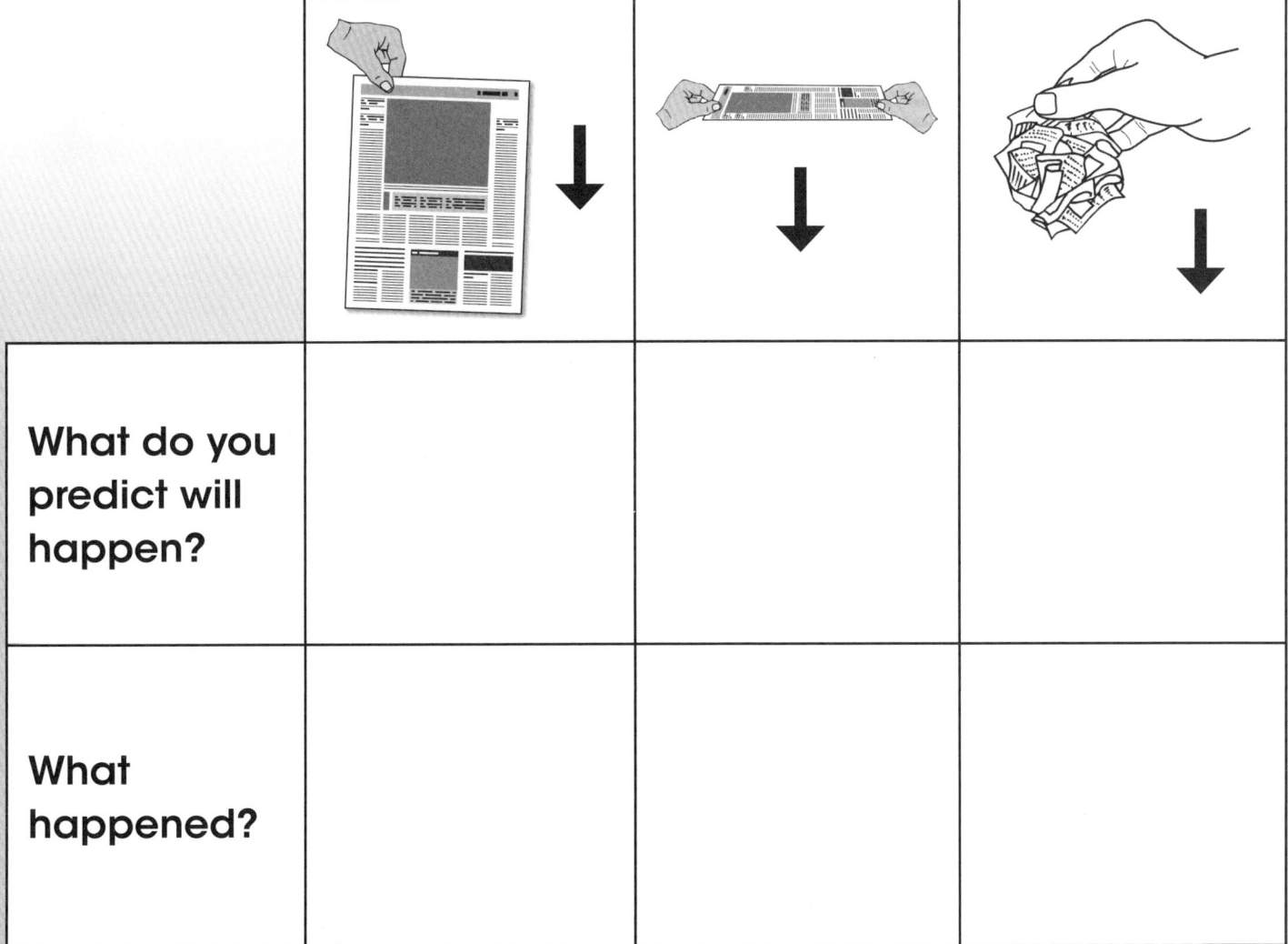

KEY FACT

When something falls, **gravity** pulls it down but it has to push air out of the way.

When the paper is smaller, it pushes less air so it falls faster.

4 Think about it!

Were your predictions right? Tick one box.

yes ☐

no ☐

some of them ☐

CHECK YOUR LEARNING

○ I know that pushes and pulls can make things go faster or slower.

6 Hearing sounds

The unit challenge

The activities in this Challenge unit will extend learners' knowledge of the following topics from the Learner's Book and Activity Book:

Topic	In this topic, learners will:
6.1 Where do sounds come from?	identify and compare the loudness of sound sources
6.2 Our ears	learn that sounds move away from the source and we hear them when they enter our ears
6.3 Sounds move	see Skills Builder, Section 6.3

Help your learner

In this unit, learners will practise making comparisons (Sections 6.1 and 6.2) and answering questions by collecting evidence through observation (Section 6.2). To help them:

1 In Section 6.2, encourage learners to listen very carefully to the quiet sounds with and without the big ear. This will be easier to do in a quiet place without other noises.

2 Help learners understand the words 'louder', 'loudest', 'quieter' and 'quietest' by reminding them of other comparative terms such as 'longer' and 'longest', 'smaller' and 'smallest'.

TEACHING TIP

Encourage learners to close their eyes when listening to sounds. This will help them to concentrate more on what they hear.

⚠ Take care with hearing activities. Very loud sounds can damage your ears.

6.1 Where do sounds come from?

listen, loud, quiet, sound, source

Loud or quiet?

1 Go outside to somewhere safe and **listen** for **loud** and **quiet** sounds.

2 Draw four sound sources from loud to quiet in the table.

Remember:
A **sound source** is something that makes a sound.

loud 	
 quiet	

CHECK YOUR LEARNING

○ I can spot loud and quiet sound sources.

⚠ Take care. Very loud sounds can damage your ears.

6.2 Our ears

soft

Do big ears help you to hear?

You will need some thin card and some sticky tape.

Look, Jamie has made a big ear.

LOOK AND LEARN

This rabbit has big ears so it can hear very **soft** sounds.

1. Roll and tape your card to make your own big ear.
2. Listen to very quiet sounds with your big ear.
3. Draw three sounds you hear.

Sound 1	Sound 2	Sound 3

4 Are the sounds louder or quieter with your big ear? Tick the correct box.

louder ☐   quieter ☐

5 Which is the loudest sound? _____

6 Which is the quietest sound? _____

7 Think about it!

Are quiet sounds easier to hear when you are close to the sound source or far away from it?

close ☐   far away ☐

CHECK YOUR LEARNING

◯ I can say when a sound is quieter or louder.

◯ I know that sounds get quieter as they move away from the sound source.

Answers

1 Being alive

1.2

Different environments

1 to **3** Answers will depend on the environments chosen and the plants and animals seen. Plants should be drawn in the plant columns, animals drawn in the animal columns.

4 Think about it!

The answer will depend on the environments chosen. (Plants are more likely to grow in environments where there is more water and more soil.)

1.3

Measure the mouse

1

2 weeks old	4 bricks
4 weeks old	6 bricks
7 weeks old	8 bricks
10 weeks old	10 bricks

2 Think about it!

gets longer?	yes ✓	no ☐
grows more fur?	yes ✓	no ☐
eats more food?	yes ✓	no ☐

1.4

Healthy and unhealthy drinks

1 Example answer: water.

2 Think about it!

Water, fizzy water and milk are all very healthy.

2 Growing plants

2.1

The life cycle of a plant

1 and **2** The learner should have drawn arrows between the stages. The missing answers might read something like those below:

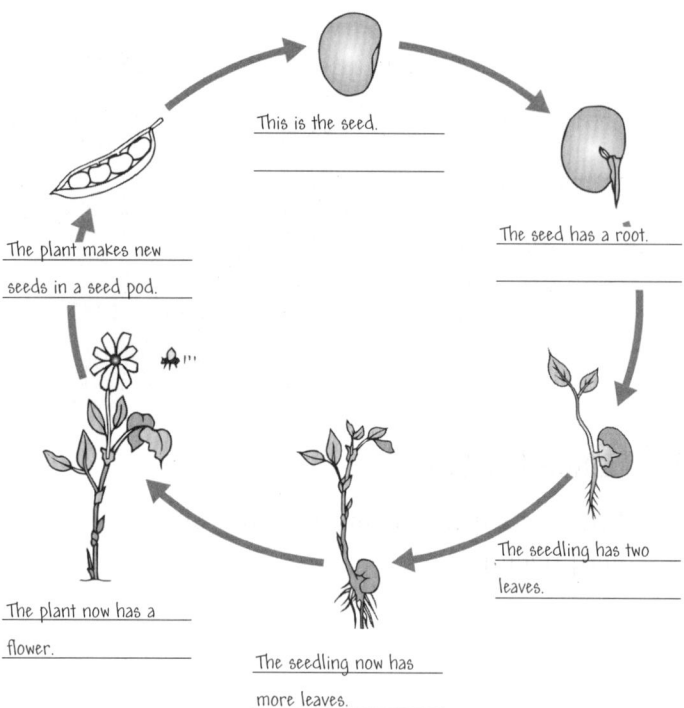

Plant foods

The learner should have drawn foods that they eat in the relevant outline, for example a carrot or sweet potato in the 'Root' outline, a chinese leaf or lettuce in the 'Leaf' outline and a banana or a pineapple in the 'Fruit' outline.

2.2

Do seeds need water?

3 to **6** The learner should have made predictions and filled in the table. It is likely that Pot 1 did not grow at all, Pot 2 grew weakly and Pot 3 grew the best. The learner should realise this is because plants need enough water to grow well.

2.3

Plants and light

1

2 and **3** The learner will draw what they will do to grow two different plants in the dark and light. If they conduct the experiment, they should realise that plants do not grow well in the dark but do better in the sunlight.

3 Ourselves

3.1

We like similar things

1 Learners should have noted a range of answers. There will be many correct responses; these are only examples:

We have similar bodies.
We all have ears.
We all have teeth.
We all get ill.
We all have hair.

We like similar foods.
We all like fruit.
We all need to drink.
We all like sweets.
We all need to eat vegetables.

We like similar games.
We all love skipping.
We love to jump.
We like to race.
We like to play in water.

We like similar stories.
We all like happy stories.
We like stories with animals.
We like funny stories.
We like traditional stories.

2 The learner should have suggested other things that they and their friends all like.

Healthy food we love

2 mango

3 orange

4 kiwi and banana

5 **Think about it!**
The learner should be able to talk about the very many ways that people are similar, for example: having similar body parts, having hair; our needs for warmth, shelter, care, food, drink; the things we love to do such as sport, games, parties, talking and so on.

3.2

Children are different

The learner should have coloured the balls that say:
We have different hair.
Some of us are tall.

3.3

Spot our body parts!

1 The learner should have correctly pointed to each of the named body parts on the picture.

2 **a** three heads

b six hands

c 30 fingers

3 **Think about it!**
Some learners will be able to name: chin, cheek, eyebrow, eyelash, eyelid, nostril, lip, skin, neck and even more.

3.4

What is this sound?

1 The learner should have filled in the first column of the table.

2 The learner should have made a prediction about which sound they think will be hardest to identify.

5 They should say any child who got all the sounds right. This should be based on the table.

6 They should identify the sound that the children had difficulty with, if there was one, and compare this with their prediction.

4 Materials in my world

4.1

Materials all around

1 The learner should have found three objects made from paper, fabric and metal. For example:
paper: wallpaper, tissue paper, newspaper
fabric: cotton or woollen clothing, towel, felt, sacking
metal: steel cutlery, cooking foil, gold jewellery

2 The learner might suggest these or others:

plastic	spoon, knife etc; toys; a household appliance e.g. radio, phone; plastic bottle
wood	table, chair, floor, picture frame, walking stick
rock	floor, wall, house
rubber	ball, tyre, eraser
glass	window, bottle, jar, light bulb, drinking glass, vase
concrete	floor, wall, step, building

3 Think about it!

The learner should suggest very useful materials. They may recognise that water is a very valuable material for life on Earth. Perhaps air is just as important?

4.2

Investigating materials

1 and **2** The learner should fill in the table based on observations.

3 The learner will say if any materials were cold to touch.

4 The learner will say if any materials were warm to touch.

5 The learner will suggest a comparative test to see if the materials are see-through, for example look through them, shine a light through them, hold them up to a window.

6 Think about it!

The learner should suggest why rubber is good for rubber bands, for example it stretches, it goes back to its first shape, it hold things tight.

4.3

Sorting with a magnet?

1 The learner will predict what they think will be pulled by the magnet in the first box.

3 The learner will draw or write their results in the second box.

4 Think about it!

The learner should talk about using the magnet to pick up the paper clips and leave the rubber bands behind. This is a form of sorting using a magnet.

5 Pushes and pulls

5.3

Pushes and pulls, big and small

1 and **2** The learner should have used the sticky notes to label things around them that need different sizes of pushes and pulls.

3 Think about it!

Big things usually need big pushes or pulls to make them move because they are heavy.

5.4

Falling paper

1 Predictions will depend on the learner's thinking.

3

What happened?	falls fast	falls slow	falls fast

4 Think about it!

The correct answer will depend on the learner's predictions.

6 Hearing sounds

6.1

Loud or quiet?

2 Answers will depend on the sounds chosen. The sounds should be in order from the loudest at the top to the quietest at the bottom.

6.2

Do big ears help you to hear?

3 Pictures drawn will depend on the sound sources chosen.

4 louder ✓

5 and **6** Answers will depend on the sounds chosen.

7 Think about it!

close ✓

Glossary

1 Being alive

animal	a living thing that can move around and eats other living things
baby	the young of an animal
compare	look at how things are similar and how they are different
drink	a liquid food
environment	a place where living things live
food	what animals eat
grow	get bigger
healthy	good for you
kitten	a baby cat, mouse, rabbit or squirrel
long/er/est	something that has two ends that are far apart
magnifying glass	shaped glass that makes objects look bigger
mouse	a very small animal with fur and a long tail
name	say what something is called
plant	a living thing that can make its own food
sugar	a very sweet food
unhealthy	not good for you
young	a baby plant or animal that has only been alive a short time

Remember: Practise saying these words aloud. Try to use them when talking about the topic.

2 Growing plants

feel	use the sense of touch to find out about something
life cycle	the different stages of an animal or plant's life, for example human baby ⟶ child ⟶ adult
light	brightness from the Sun; plants need light
seed	the part of a plant from which a new plant can grow
seedling	a very young plant with about two leaves
stage	one part of an animal or plant's life cycle, for example childhood
water	liquid that plants need to grow

Glossary

3 Ourselves

body	the whole part of a person or animal
different	not the same
hear	you hear sounds using your ears
pictogram	a way of showing something with pictures
see	to look at things with your eyes
senses	the things animals use to find out about the world around them
similar	being the same in some ways
smell	you use your nose to smell things
taste	you taste your food using your tongue
tongue	the part of your mouth that helps you to feel and taste food
touch	a sense you use to feel things

4 Materials in my world

Remember: Practise saying these words aloud. Try to use them when talking about the topic.

concrete	a mixture of water, sand and cement that goes hard like a rock
elastic	stretchy
fabric	a soft, flexible material used to make clothes and other things
flexible	when something can bend easily
glass	a material that you can see through
magnet	an object that pulls some metals towards it
materials	we use materials like glass, wood, plastic and fabric to make many things that we use every day
metal	a material that is often strong and shiny
paper	a material that you use to write on
plastic	a type of material that may be coloured
properties	the words we use to describe a material
rock	hard material found in the ground
rough	bumpy, not flat
rubber	a material that can bend easily and keeps water out
see-through	clear or very thin so you can see through it, like glass
smooth	flat, not bumpy
soft	gentle to touch, not hard
sort	put things into groups
strong	powerful, not easily broken
test	do something to see what happens
wood	a material that comes from the trunk of a tree

5 Pushes and pulls

fall	to go downwards when not held up
fast/er/est	taking a short time to get to another place
gravity	a force that pulls everything down to the ground
move/ing/ment	change position
predict	to say what might happen
pull	try to move something towards you
push	try to move something away from you
slow/er/est	taking a long time to get to another place

6 Hearing sounds

listen	you use your ears to listen to sounds
loud/er/est	a sound that makes a lot of noise
quiet/er/est	a sound that only makes a little noise
soft	a quiet sound
sound	something you can hear
source	where something comes from or where it is made